Creating Mindful Moments

Sandra Harwood

"Cultivate your inner strength and wisdom
through creating mindful moments
and gently shifting your inner dialogue."
- Sandra Harwood -

Some Reflections on Creating Mindful Moments ...

"Reading *Creating Mindful Moments* has helped me notice the way I talk to myself and others. It has given me useful tools and ideas to create more peaceful and positive interactions with myself and those around me. Sandra's honest and down to earth examples show how easy and effective this practice can be."

— **Genevieve Jones**

"This book has opened my mind to delving deeper into the words used by myself and those around me. Sandra has articulated an idea that has set itself on the periphery for many years, that 'language matters' – the language we use to communicate with others, as well as that we use to communicate with ourselves.

"Through simple and practical methods and short exercises for the mind, this book has helped me unlock a deeper understanding of the relationships I have formed with myself, my family, friends and work colleagues.

"*Creating Mindful Moments* is essentially a toolkit that many people will find themselves revisiting as their own Mindful journey evolves."

— **Matthew Vitoli**

"'Mindfulness'" is the catchphrase of the moment, to the point where it is almost meaningless. Sandra's book, *Creating Mindful Moments*, unpacks in a very accessible way how looking inwards at our thoughts, words and listening to our body we can live a more content, peaceful life and enjoy better relationships."

    –Melissa Fowler

"Through relatable, real-life examples, *Creating Mindful Moments* has set the foundations to allow me to become more aware of my inner-dialogue, the way it affects my actions and the way I interact with those around me. In addition, the pauses and meditations gave me time to reflect and be more mindful."

    – Jessica Gallitto

"I was unsure about how this book was going to help or benefit me in everyday life, as l didn't have a great love for self-assessment.

"I found the book to be written with such sincerity and honesty that it had me captivated from the moment l opened up the first page. I felt like l wanted to get to know the author for her genuine nature and ability to capture the very essence of my feelings. It had me thinking about how to resolve situations in an appropriate manner, how to respect others as well as myself and how to enjoy every waking moment regardless of how big or small they are.

"I really enjoyed reading *Creating Mindful Moments*."

    – Angela Santi

"In *Creating Mindful Moments*, Sandra has shared her very personal journey of mindfulness, which has included times of despair and heartbreak, as well as moments of joy and accomplishment.

"When reading *Creating Mindful Moments*, I found myself answering the questions posed and being able relate so clearly to the examples provided. Since then I have found opportunities to pause, question and challenge my own inner dialogue and outward actions.

"*Creating Mindful Moments* was very easy to read and was filled with suggestions that acknowledge that although our lives are busy, there are always opportunities for mindful moments and positive thoughts. A wonderfully practical resource that can be read all in one go, or savoured chapter by chapter."
     – Colleen Mahoney

"In our world with its innumerable distractions, stressors and challenges, we are all striving to find ways to find some breathing room and be in the present moment.

"Through beautiful simplicity, and sharing her touching, lived experience, Sandra Harwood gives us the tools, strategies and insight into bringing a calmness, harmony and more time into our bustling schedules. The lessons contained in this book are artfully communicated and accompanied with elegant, practical exercises aimed at developing a deeper connection with the reader's world through the practice of mindfulness.

"A beautiful and lovingly crafted literary work that allows the reader to unlock their own mindful moments and breathe deeply in their busy lives."
     – Denis Johnstone

First published by Busybird Publishing 2017
Copyright © 2017 Sandra Harwood

ISBN
Print: 978-1-925692-03-7
Ebook: 978-1-925692-04-4

Sandra Harwood has asserted her right under the Copyright, Designs and Patents Act 1988 to be identified as the author of this work. The information in this book is based on the author's experiences and opinions. The publisher specifically disclaims responsibility for any adverse consequences, which may result from use of the information contained herein. Permission to use information has been sought by the author. Any breaches will be rectified in further editions of the book.

All rights reserved. No part of this publication may be reproduced, stored in or introduced into a retrieval system, or transmitted in any form, or by any means (electronic, mechanical, photocopying, recording or otherwise) without the prior written permission of the author. Any person who does any unauthorised act in relation to this publication may be liable to criminal prosecution and civil claims for damages. Enquiries should be made through the publisher.

Cover image: Jane Power
Cover design: Busybird Publishing
Layout and typesetting: Busybird Publishing
Editor: Lauren Magee

Busybird Publishing
2/118 Para Road
Montmorency, Victoria
Australia 3094
www.busybird.com.au

Disclaimer: This book is in no way intended as a substitute for professional or individual advice in any way. You should consult with the appropriate qualified professional – psychologists, psychiatrists, counsellors, medical practitioners, and other healthcare providers – for any advice relating to your particular needs and circumstances.

The names in the book have been changed to protect the privacy of participants who shared their experiences.

I dedicate this book to my daughters, Eden and Eloise.

You have both inspired me to do my best

and enriched my life in different ways.

Contents

Introduction	i
How This Book Is Structured	v

Chapter 1
Concept: Inviting Mindful Moments	1
Language Shift: Emotions As Indicators	7
Task To Promote Emotions as Indicators	10
A Mindful Moment: Exploring Our Values	12

Chapter 2
Concept: Setting Intentions	13
Language Shift: I Choose	19
Task To Support Choices	21
A Mindful Moment: Just As I Am	23

Chapter 3
Concept: Sharing Experiences Harmoniously	25
Language Shift: Get Specific	28
Task To Support Being Specific	30
A Mindful Moment: Inviting New Pathways	32

Chapter 4
Concept: Embracing Comfort And Discomfort	33
Language Shift: What's Happening Here?	38
Task To Discover What Is Happening	40
A Mindful Moment: Noticing What's Happening	43

Chapter 5
Concept: Exploring Compassion	45
Language Shift: Expand our Perspectives	49
Task Promoting Expanding our Perspectives	51
A Mindful Moment: Cultivating Compassion	53

Chapter 6
    Concept: Beyond Thoughts   55
    Language Shift: What Am I Willing To Do?   59
    Task To Support Values   60
    A Mindful Moment: Self-Respect   64

Chapter 7
    Concept: Bringing New Light To Positive And Negative   65
    Language Shift: Win-Win Thinking Patterns   70
    Task To Support Win-Win Thinking   74
    A Mindful Moment: Clarity   76

Chapter 8
    Concept: Peaceful Connections   77
    Language Shift: Checking In   83
    Task Supporting Checking In   85
    A Mindful Moment: Peaceful Connections   87

Conclusion   89

Acknowledgements   93

About the Author   97

Recommended Resources
    Books   99
    Audio book   100
    Websites   100
    Lecture   101
    Videos   101
    App   101

Introduction

"Defining yourself through thought is limiting yourself."
- Eckhart Tolle -

A calm centre exists in all of us. It only takes the desire to listen to ourselves with compassion and an open mind to discover we are all our own peacekeepers.

Our thoughts give us an insight into who we are, however there is more to us than just thoughts. To build our personal strength, it is essential we focus on developing our skills through awareness, acceptance and compassion.

This book has been written to highlight the need and opportunity to create mindful moments in our day. Taking a moment to oneself and tapping into our inner-stillness can provide greater clarity, which can be especially helpful in tough times.

We have the ability to surf life's ups and downs and to manage suffering with a sense of harmony; I would love this vision to be more accessible, as I feel a more peaceful existence is possible.

The strategies explored in this book are intended to support our emotional, intellectual and physical health. Desired outcomes include:

- Empowering connections with self and others
- Discovering our strongest, wisest and most peaceful self.

To achieve these outcomes, we will practice:

- Developing awareness of our current inner dialogue
- Taking regular pauses to support connection with ourselves and others
- Developing inner-strength whilst observing our breath
- Adapting our dialogue to enhance awareness
- Improving our ability to respond with extra consideration for self and others.

A key turning point in my life was when I was 36 weeks pregnant and lost my first baby, Eden. She was stillborn. After such heartbreak, returning to work as a teacher in the surrounds of gorgeous children and families was more challenging than I had imagined. I was determined to enjoy my professional work and re-build other areas of myself, while I "managed" my grief. I am grateful for the support of family, friends, colleagues, Mercy for Women's hospital staff and counsellors who helped me heal, cultivate inner-strength and grow from my experience.

Linda, my coach and mentor at the time, supported my personal quest to discover and explore strategies that could transform suffering into strengths. I am thankful that she went beyond her duties and encouraged me to share my resources with colleagues. This greatly improved my confidence and my feeling of self-worth. I was able to

Introduction

develop a new sense of connection and purpose, which was just what I needed then.

Four years later I gave birth to my second daughter, Eloise. I am now enjoying the experience of being a mum physically, not just being a mum in my heart. My search for inner-strength has given me the ability to tap into inner-peace and a sense of harmony with self and others. My quest for a more peaceful existence is ongoing as life throws continuous curve balls to ensure we evolve.

In this fast-moving world, we frequently find ourselves in autopilot; we are ruled by our reactive thoughts and actions as we hurry from one activity to another. Research shows that practicing mindfulness and building our ability to be present, helps us increase our over all wellbeing. Increasing our awareness improves the way we respond to stress and the way we manage our life. Being able to press pause in our day enables us to listen and understand ourselves, and each other more effectively, and enriches our connections and quality of life. On this note, I welcome you on your unique journey to finding your inner peace and wisdom.

How This Book Is Structured

"Focus on clarifying what is being observed, felt, and needed rather than on diagnosing and judging."

- Marshall Rosenberg -

New Concepts

Each chapter introduces a *concept*, which is based on my own discoveries around mindfulness practices. The concepts are devised to bring clarity to our thoughts and actions as we reflect on our current level of wellness. Moreover, it helps us discover our inner wisdom, strength and peacekeeper.

Mindfulness is not something we can know – it is a practice. Like daily flossing helps keep our teeth healthy, mindfulness helps keep our mind healthy too. The process of taking time to notice whether our thoughts or feelings are in the past or future, and bringing our attention back to the present moment, is a skill that can strengthen the way our brain works and how our brain communicates with the rest of our body. The more often we practice bringing our attention into the present moment, the sharper our instincts and thought processes are. This also increases our ability to live more harmoniously.

Each of us is our own expert. We can bounce ideas, share experiences and support each other, however, we are ultimately accountable for our own wellbeing. We have the natural capacity to care for ourselves and yet we may often push ourselves until we are unwell; being accountable for our own wellbeing improves the way we care for ourselves. Examples are used throughout the book to support each concept. Although some examples refer to conversations we may have with others, the main emphasis in this book is on the way we speak to ourselves first.

> "This world is what we have made of it. If it is ruthless today it is because we have made it ruthless by our attitudes. If we change ourselves we can change the world, and changing ourselves begins with changing our language and methods of communication."
>
> - Arun Gandhi -

The Language Shifts

Each concept in this book is supported by a *language shift*. These suggestions are developed to equip us with the tools to find our own words. We do this through:

- Recognising hidden pain behind words
- Developing healthy ways to hear and console ourselves
- Empowering ourselves through adapting our language, so we can move forward with strength.

As a teacher, I have taken part in a variety of Professional Development. A stand out was a workshop about the *Drama Triangle*. In brief, the *Drama Triangle* is about roles we chose to play-out in a conflict situation: the victim (martyr), the antagonist (bully) or the hero. I believe these roles can obscure our capacity to care for each other and ourselves. These roles often hide unresolved pain, discomfort, anger, sadness, frustration, mistrust or even just plain awkwardness.

For example: When I first decided to write this book I could hear myself saying, "I don't want others to suffer like I have. I will teach people how to treat themselves, because none of us know how to … "

Let's take a closer look at this statement:

- "I don't want others to suffer like I have." This could be victim-type thinking.
- "I will teach people how to treat themselves better." This could be hero-type thinking.
- " … because none of us know how to … " This could be antagonistic-type thinking.

As you can see, it is possible to have all three roles playing in one thought process. Although there is much compassion for self and others behind this statement, when I looked deeper, there was unresolved pain.

To move beyond this unresolved pain I needed to:

- Accept that pain is part of the journey
- Take into account our ability to heal ourselves
- Be accountable for my contribution to my own pain
- Explore strategies to help transform pain into strength and purpose
- Share my experiences in a way that supports others in their own journey.

Example above rephrased: "I write as a means to help manage the natural suffering that is part of our journey, so I can grow and develop my strengths and ability to surf life's inevitable ups and downs. I enjoy sharing experiences and opportunities, that support others with the same intention, to strive for a more peaceful existence."

Although drama roles are natural human reactions, they are part of our basic survival system, whereas well-considered responses are more complex and take into account the over all wellbeing of others and ourselves. The three roles either push, pull or handball accountability, often avoiding our real issues. Just noticing our automatic reactions to any situation can help us bypass the drama roles. We can build awareness of our inner-dialogue and intentions by asking ourselves questions like:

- Am I focused on connection or judging?
- Am I aiming to interact or control?
- Am I being accountable, blaming or handballing?

When we are judging, controlling, blaming or handballing, we are usually attempting to squash or avoid pain.

For example: "She has made me so angry because she just doesn't understand I am trying to help." This is most likely victim type thinking; it indicates that someone else has control over how I feel and act. Although we cannot control how others treat us, we can manage the way we respond.

When we are connecting, interacting and being accountable, we are allowing pain and vulnerability to surface and therefore we are able to resolve situations with extra clarity.

For example: "This situation is so frustrating because we don't understand each other yet." This second example allows for equal accountability and understanding. It also allows for compassion and opportunities to find clear solutions.

When we *truly* wish others well, it is difficult to judge them and we are less likely to be judged. Developing this ruthless well-wishing attitude increases our ability to be accepting and open to other viewpoints. It also enhances our perceptions, strengthens our mind and our ability to communicate effectively.

Focusing on connecting with others' needs and holding your needs *equally* is a balancing act worth practicing. The balance of both yours and another's needs creates awareness and opens doors to build rewarding connections.

Language shifts are a process of listening with kindness and adapting our current inner-dialogue to enable more conscious thought processes. When we increase our awareness of word choices we also increase our ability to empower our connections through mutually respectful dialogue. It is this mutually respectful inner-dialogue that will support a more peaceful existence.

> "By simply pondering and affirming your deepest values you'll improve the health of your brain, you'll protect yourself from burnout at work, you'll reduce your propensity to ruminate about failure, and you'll be less reactive and defensive when someone confronts you with uncomfortable information."
>
> - Andrew Newberg, M.D. -

Tasks

The *tasks* are designed to "try on" concepts and language shifts. The practice of accepting and acknowledging our current thought patterns can help us clear our mind. Once we practice these tasks, our minds tend to find more supportive strategies towards hearing our wise inner voice. The amount of times we use these exercises will depend on our individual needs.

At present, reward and punishment is our main currency when developing new skills.

For example: If I eat something unhealthy, I may scold myself to prevent myself from repeating this behaviour. If someone treats us poorly, we may respond equally poorly to show this behaviour is unacceptable.

Although this method appears reasonable, it often has long-term side effects that distract us from enriching our understanding of self and others.

For example: Rather than scolding myself for eating unhealthy food, I could look for equally enjoyable foods that are healthy. Instead of treating others poorly, I could set clear boundaries to prevent someone treating me that way again.

I aim to support our deeper values and our most authentic selves. These practices develop our ability to enjoy the present moment, minus the long-term side effects that dwelling in the past or worrying about the future give us. This does take time, repetition and a willingness to adapt, however the challenge is well worthwhile.

> "One conscious breath can bring you back in contact with yourself and the world around you."
>
> - Barbara Ann Kipfer -

A Mindful Moment

Interlacing mini-mind-breaks in our day opens avenues to enhance our wellbeing. The *mindful moments* have been created to support our ability to make empowering changes in the way we approach life. By planting encouraging thoughts, over time, we can build a friendlier relationship with ourselves; they are stepping stones towards meditation and hearing our calm inner voice.

Creating moments in our day gives us a chance to check in with ourselves, notice our thoughts, emotions and sensations, as we support our wellbeing. Once we begin the practice of pausing, we can weave clarity and peace into our day. This enables us to expand our available strategies towards more effective pathways in our lives.

Feel free to adapt the *mindful moments* so they meet your needs. Alternatively, you may simply choose to take a moment's pause to reflect, as a strategy to support your wellbeing whenever needed. A mini-break can be as informal as, *I am aware of my breath.*

One of my clients made a photocopy of each mindful moment and used them for one week each. She said this worked really well for her.

You may choose to record yourself reading the *mindful moments* and play them back to yourself when needed. For extra support, I have created recorded versions of the *mindful moments* for you to access via website: creatingmindfulmoments.com

> "If you take a moment to pull yourself into the present moment, these old negative voices will lose their power."
>
> - Andrew Newberg, M.D., and Mark Robert Waldman -

Chapter 1

Concept: Inviting Mindful Moments

Courtesy of Luke Purchase and Irene Cornerstone (12 Moons Today).

> "Mindful awareness is waking up to what's happening inside of you, and in the world, moment by moment."
>
> - Mark Williams and Danny Penman -

Being aware of the present moment is a practice that invites a sense of peace. Accessing our "sensing mode" (e.g. awareness of our breath, physical selves, sounds, sight, smells, taste, movement, thoughts, emotions and surroundings) helps support our ability to experience life in the moment, rather than experiencing life through thought. As an added bonus, it also helps us relax.

Being relaxed and calm increases our chances of making informed choices. We also increase our potential to enjoy life, in light of our ups and downs. To build our awareness we can focus on our senses. Examples of inviting mindful moments are:

- Noticing if our breath is shallow, deep, smooth, irregular, fast or slow
- Observing if our body feels tense or relaxed
- Focusing on sounds within our body, like our heart or our breath
- Looking around us and noticing something we hadn't noticed
- Smelling our food, with our eyes closed, and savoring at least one bite
- Closing our eyes and giving our full attention to one sip of a beverage
- Walking slowly whilst observing our feet from heel to toe with each step
- Washing our hands and noticing the feel of the water and the smell of the soap.

Chapter 1

Meditation is a great way to find calm; it supports our mind, body and spirit to heal, grow and develop. Meditation creates a window of peace to help us see situations more clearly and physically improves our wellbeing.

Directing our attention to one or two breaths can be a *mini-meditation* towards relaxing and calming our mind and body. To take this further, we can string a few focused breaths together, building our ability to calm our mind and increase awareness. This assists us to interrupt unhelpful thoughts and behaviour patterns, so we can create more empowering choices.

> "... how we decide to live our lives, and in essence, how we decide to keep our minds, actually changes not just our ideas and our opinions and how caught we get in them, but actually changes our relationship to thought. And then when we look at the structure of the brain, not only is the brain functioning differently, but the actual structure of the brain ... is being recruited into greater use in compassion, equanimity, clarity and wisdom."
>
> - Jon Kabat-Zinn -

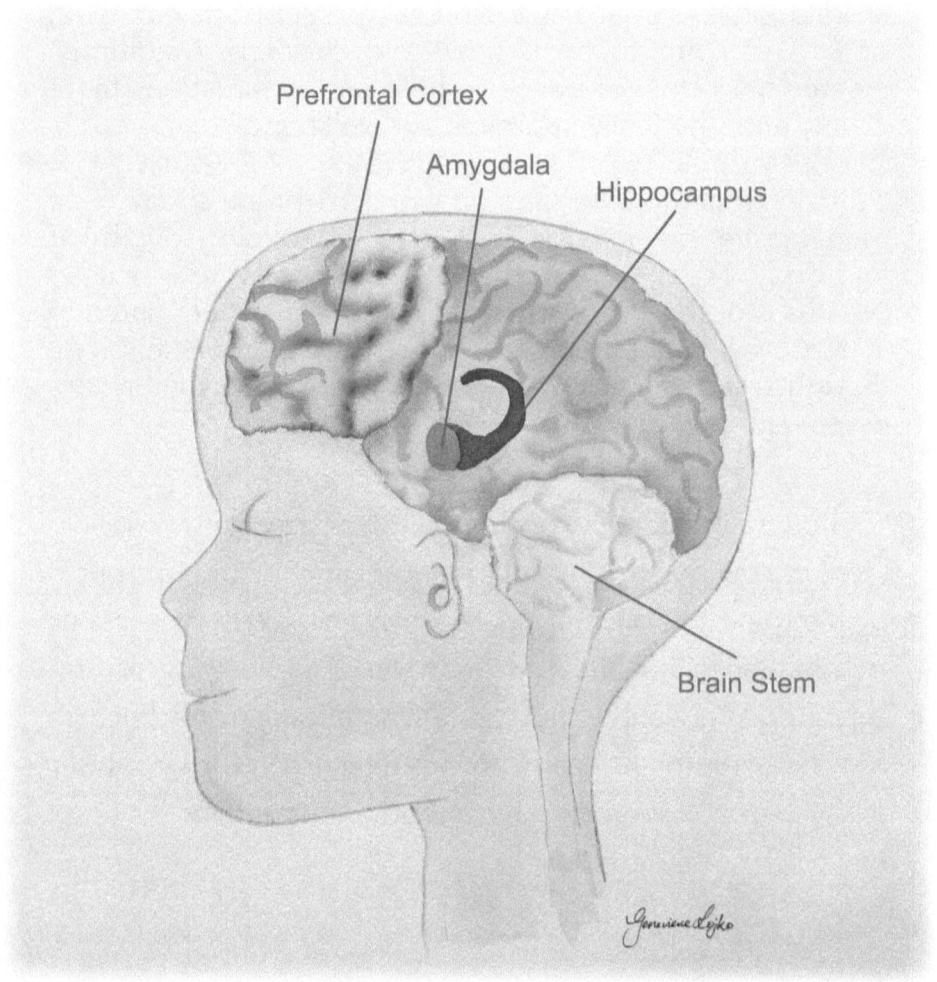

Image courtesy of Genevieve Lojko.

A very brief overview of four areas of our brain will give us just enough information to help notice the difference between our automatic reactions, and well-considered responses. Although our brain has a great range of complex functions, its main objective is to keep us alive.

1. Our Brainstem is located at the base of our brain. It looks after all the automatic survival mechanisms that we don't need to think about, like breathing, heartbeat and digestion.

2. Our Prefrontal Cortex (PFC) is situated in the upper front area of our brain. Our PFC processes our most advanced skills like problem solving, impulse control, logic, morals, empathy, virtues, understanding, compassion and integrity. When we are calm, we can access this area of the brain to gain insight and form well-considered responses.
3. Our Amygdala is like an internal alarm. It is part of our limbic system (middle brain) also known as our emotional brain. Our amygdala is triggered when we sense an imminent threat; it can be a real threat, like a car coming towards us, or a perceived threat like someone ignoring us. This is when our fight, flight or freeze mode kicks in; it shuts down connections to our PFC so that our body gets extra oxygen and energy to protect ourselves. For extra support, adrenalin and cortisol hormones are also released into our body, though this is only helpful when we are in real danger.
4. Our Hippocampus is also part of our emotional brain. It is where our most important memories are stored. It is important to note that our memories can trigger our amygdala as well.

For us to have a more harmonious approach to life's ups and downs, we need to be aware of when we are being triggered by extreme emotions, so we can respond with more insight.

Have you ever said or done something to hurt someone and then later thought *Why did I do that*? When we experience uncomfortable emotions, such as high volumes of anger, rejection, hopelessness, frustration and sadness, our amygdala is triggered and switches off connection to our higher thinking. When we experience comfortable emotions like love, appreciation, gratitude and kindness, our brain feels safe and therefore we can think more clearly and access more insightful responses. Positive emotions release valuable hormones called endorphins, dopamine, oxytocin and serotonin. These enjoyable feelings can also have long-term healing effects for our body, brain and spirit.

Emotions are chemical messages sent between our brain and body to help keep us safe. When we become aware that this communication system is trying to protect us, we can create an opportunity to listen with extra consideration to what our brain and body is trying to tell us.

Taking a moment to calm down when we are experiencing extreme levels of emotion can help us notice our automatic reactions, giving us insight towards our real needs and values. A moment of reflection can help us form more considered responses.

Awareness of our breath can increase the amount of oxygen going to our brain and assists our calm and wise thought processes. It maximises our ability to invite a moment of clarity. By practicing staying calm at times we already feel safe, we prepare and build improved paths in our brain. It also enables us to have better access to our higher thinking when we experience extreme emotions.

> "These people—the ones with a joyful amygdala—are more focused on promoting the good than on preventing the bad. This is called an 'approach orientation' which has numerous benefits for physical and mental health, relationships, and success."
>
> - Rick Hanson -

The practice of noticing and enjoying moments of happiness throughout the day can help us re-wire our brain and help us develop a "joyful amygdala" too. Hanson suggests that we take at least "20 to 30 seconds" to enjoy a positive experience. This could be a simple as enjoying a bite of your meal, a sip of a beverage, a peaceful sound, something in nature, a hug or a compliment. He says that making efforts to notice enjoyable moments approximately six times a day can help us build resilience and increase our over all wellbeing. This helps us to be less dependent on external fulfillment and more able to feel self-fulfilled. As we develop our ability to self-manage our thoughts, emotions and responses, we build our ability to find and create our own joy.

Language Shift: Emotions As Indicators

Some emotions can leave us feeling stuck in reactive modes. We can choose to express our emotions in a way that leaves us feeling trapped, or we can express them in a way that empowers us. By reframing the way we express our emotions, we can use them as indicators of our needs. This is an opportunity for a language shift that can help us discover directions that will support our values.

To help us observe situations more clearly, we need a space between emotions and actions. We can do this by listening carefully to our emotions, minus the surface behaviours. Shifting our language can enable this process.

For example: When we hear ourselves make statements like, "They make me angry", "He makes me sad", "She always does this to me", our emotions are trying to tell us we are not comfortable and something needs to change. By reframing our thoughts we can invite a clear direction. When we add, "I notice" before expressing the emotion, we acknowledge how we feel and give ourselves the space to process what is happening and create a more supportive moment.

For example:

- I notice I am feeling sad; I am going to talk to a friend.
- I notice I am feeling awkward; I will go for a walk to re-set.
- I notice I am feeling angry; I will take three breaths to help me calm down.
- I notice I am feeling uncomfortable; I will do something else until I am calm enough to try again.

Re-framing the way we express our emotions creates a clear connection to the higher-thinking areas of our brain. This space enables us to use our emotions as an indicator of what we need to do to feel safe, healthy, comfortable, understood or appreciated. It assists us to direct our behaviour and communicate our needs more clearly and supports our preferred focus and path in life. Once we have made space for a supportive moment, we can take "20 to 30 seconds" to appreciate the window of positivity we have created.

Often we may feel the need to blame others for the situation we are in. If we focus on blaming others for everything, we will miss out on building our strength through being accountable. Accountability facilitates us to feel empowered. When we discover the part of a situation we are accountable for, we can choose to change our thought patterns and actions as we encourage more valuable interactions with others.

A major player in our language is the subtle "I want" statement. These statements sound innocent and harmless. To expose the trap "I want" statements can create, I invite you to read the following out loud and notice the difference once we shift them to "I prefer", "I like", "I love", and "I would enjoy".

Chapter 1

I want	I prefer, like, love or enjoy
I want my family to be loving.	I enjoy when my family is being loving.
I want my friends to understand me.	I love it when my friends understand me.
I want my own space.	I prefer my own space.
I want to be financially free.	I would enjoy being financially free.

When we say "I want", it means that we are feeling stuck or insufficient; I never had it, or had it once and no longer have it, and I cannot be happy until I get it.

When we hear statements that begin with "I want", it gives us an indication that we are most likely not in a good place at that moment.

In contrast, words like "I prefer", "I like", "I love", and "I would enjoy" give us a direction to work towards. It expresses that "I understand myself" and a sense of, "it is possible for me to fulfill my own needs one way or another". This type of language keeps our amygdala calm, enabling us to access our insights, which will open doors to new mindful pathways.

"If you intensely focus on words like 'peace' or 'love', the emotional centres of the brain calm down ... by using language to help us reflect on positive ideas and emotions, we can enhance our overall wellbeing and improve the function of our brain."

- Andrew Newberg, M.D, and Mark Robert Waldman -

To help check if our choices are supporting us, we can take a moment to focus on our breath as we ask ourselves:

- Are my thoughts and actions helpful, safe, healthy and comfortable?
- Is this situation helpful, safe, healthy and comfortable?
- What would I enjoy, like, love or prefer in this situation?

By exploring our responses to these questions, we will discover our preferred thoughts and actions in any situation. Understanding our needs and values increases our ability to find more insightful options towards a peaceful existence.

Task To Promote Emotions as Indicators

To redirect new pathways, write down your uncomfortable thoughts, emotions or situations on the left side of the page.

As an alternative to struggling with the negatives in life, this task helps us to highlight the positive direction we would prefer to move towards.

On the right side, write down the opposite. This will help uncover what your emotions are indicating and will enable you to work towards meeting your needs and values.

Uncomfortable Thoughts, Emotions or Situations	Opposite (What would I prefer, I like, I love, I would enjoy?)
e.g.	e.g.
I don't have time to clean	I prefer a clean environment
I keep dropping everything	I enjoy being safe
I am frustrated when rushed	I like a calm pace
I want them to listen	I love clear communication
I should be able to stay calm	I love being calm

You can take this task one step further by using your discoveries to improve considered and informed inner-dialogue and responses.

Use the statement "At the same time" to mutually respect both your uncomfortable and preferred thoughts and actions (e.g. I don't have time to clean. At the same time, I prefer a clean environment. I am willing to clean the main areas for one hour each week, and get help with the rest).

_____

_____

_____

_____

A Mindful Moment: Exploring Our Values

Begin by finding space to pause

For just a moment
I allow myself to feel free from the past
Free from anything that could happen
I take a break from life, as I know it

In this moment
I choose to focus on how I feel
With the intention
To discover my values

My values include the feelings
That support my wellbeing
Like respect, freedom,
Peace, and love

As I follow my breath in, and out,
I accept any emotions that arise
And acknowledge the genuine support
My feelings are trying to give me

I allow my values to float calmly
Around and within me
Guiding my thoughts,
Attitude, and actions

Breathing in, and out,
As I prepare to re-enter my daily life.

Chapter 2

Concept: Setting Intentions

Image courtesy of Luke Purchase and Irene Cornerstone (12 Moons Today).

> "Instead of habitual, automatic reactions, our words become conscious responses based firmly on awareness of what we are perceiving, feeling and wanting."
> - Marshall Rosenberg -

This chapter requires us to keep in mind our brain's main function is to keep us alive. Our automatic reactions are helpful if we are in real danger, but unhelpful if we are not. The base and mid-brain focus on immediate survival needs, whereas our prefrontal cortex is able to consider our short-term and long-term wellbeing and that of others.

Our automatic responses are often laced with unhelpful language that conceals our real pain. This disempowers us, as it distracts us from finding meaningful intentions like being heard, respected, acknowledged, and appreciated. Responses such as "How dare you!" or "Who do you think you are?" aim to protect us, however they sound threatening and can set off our amygdala; these words will most likely trigger others around you too, activating everyone's basic survival mode of *fight, flight* or *freeze*.

When we listen beyond our automatic thoughts and reactions, we gain insight towards how to meet our real needs and values. Here are some examples and possible translations:

- "How dare you!" translates to, "That hurt, I'm in disbelief. I need a moment to process what just happened and figure out what to do next".
- "Who do you think you are?" translates to, "I thought I understood you, now I don't know what to say or what to think. I need some time to reflect before responding".

- "I should have done it differently", translates to, "I regret this happened, as this doesn't match what I intended. I would like to try again".
- "They have no idea", "No one ever listens", "No one understands", translates to, "I would like to be acknowledged, heard, respected, accepted and appreciated".
- "I have no choice", "It's all their fault", "Why is this happening to me?" translates to, "This is out of control. I would like more choice or I would like things to be different".

The translations help us identify and acknowledge our pain before our emotions snowball. Understanding one's self prevents us from getting defensive and saying things that will cause us and others more harm. More importantly, these translations help us uncover our real intentions such as keeping us safe, healthy, respected and free to be ourselves.

> "We've got this negativity bias that's a kind of bug in the stone-age brain in the 21st century ... It makes it hard for us to learn from our positive experiences, even though learning from your positive experiences is the primary way to grow inner strength."
>
> - Dr. Rick Hanson -

Before we go into developing intentions, it is important to note Dr. Hanson's work. His research shows that our brains have more neurons that pick up on negative experiences than those that pick up on positive experiences. This is also a part of our brains protection and survival mode. His work on promoting and developing our own "self-directed neuroplasticity" inspired me to take more notice of my automatic responses. I love that there is evidence that we can self-direct and re-wire our brains towards increasing our wellbeing and inner-peace.

> "In relationships it typically takes five good interactions to make up for a single bad one".
>
> - Rick Hanson -

When our brain brings up past danger or possible future danger, our brain and body may respond as if it's happening to us right now. If our thoughts are constantly setting off our amygdala, then we can cause ourselves unnecessary suffering.

I have often heard myself say things like, "What is wrong with me?" or "Of course I mucked up again!" One hundred good things could happen to me, then one thing goes wrong, and that's all I think about. When something goes wrong, I tend to start bringing up all the things that ever went wrong in my life, or could ever go wrong in the future; a very unhelpful snowball effect that leaves me feeling immobile and unable to think clearly.

To prevent this unwarranted suffering, I would like to combine Newberg and Waldman's advice to "pull yourself into the present moment" and extend Dr. Hanson's "five to one" ratio into daily practices; when possible, if we find we are in an unwanted situation, we can look for five positive experiences at that moment to help connect us to our brains higher thinking areas.

To further heal and increase our abilities, we can notice which thoughts are from the past or trying to predict the future; guiding ourselves back to the present moment prevents us from getting attached to our thoughts. By taking a couple of deep breaths and noticing our thoughts, emotions and physical body, we bring ourselves back to this moment. This helps us to relax.

For some time, one of my automatic thought patterns was "I am clumsy". When I was a child, I was affectionately called clumsy, so I accepted the trait. I thought that was the way I was and would always be. I was also influenced by comedy shows that had clumsy main characters. As a result, I was stuck with this thought pattern all the way into my forties. Now that I take time to be aware, comfort myself and am able to set intentions, I take better care of myself. As a result, I have less clumsy moments.

For example: As I try to get all my bags for work into the car, I bump my head on the roof of the car. I would notice how I feel, and respond with "I know, that hurt! Although I am in a hurry, I realise I would prefer to be safe, so I choose to slow down".

Setting intentions is one way we can support self-directing our thoughts and actions. Positive thought processes, including being optimistic, encouraging, grateful and kind, enhance our brain's function and impacts on our life. This means that we notice what makes us uncomfortable, discover what we would prefer, and use that information to set intentions.

Here are some examples of intentions you could set. "I will":

- Build more respectful connections
- Increase consideration for self and others equally
- Transform old pain into new strengths
- Cultivate unconditional love for self and others
- Introduce healthy and encouraging thought patterns

- Re-distribute my time so that my needs are supported
- Choose to spend extra time with compassionate people
- Increase awareness of harmonious strategies.

Our values help us listen beyond our thoughts. When we live by our values we are able to balance our mind, body and spirit. What are your core values?

To help you begin exploring, here are some examples – love, health, safety, respect, harmony, integrity, clarity, innovation, humour, contribution, cooperation, courage, determination, ease, loyalty, patience, creativity, authenticity, freedom, spontaneity, fun, tradition or understanding.

To find an intention that meets our values and put it into action we can:

- *Listen beyond thoughts.* Take a moment to accept yourself and the current situation as it is. Check your thoughts, emotions and physical responses (e.g. When I am working on the computer too long, my thoughts sound clunky and my shoulders feel tight).
- *Observe values and intentions.* Listen to your discomfort with the purpose of discovering what you value most at this moment and allow your true intention to surface (e.g. I value my health and intend to respect my body and mind).
- *Notice any calm responses that arise.* Repeat your values and intentions in your mind and listen for your inner wisdom (e.g. I am really not comfortable, and this does not feel healthy. I will take a break and do something else for a few minutes – stretch, walk, drink a glass of water. I will reassess before continuing. This will ensure clear thoughts, a relaxed body and respect for the work I would like to produce).

Chapter 2

Language Shift: I Choose

"Worthiness doesn't have prerequisites."

- Brené Brown -

Autopilot is referring to our "automatic responses" in any situation. Pausing to notice our breath can be the first step towards making more considerate decisions leading to fewer regrets.

We can reset our autopilot by setting a foundation for worthiness. To support this we will shift the words "I deserve" to "I choose". How much judging is going on when we use the word deserve? And who is the authority telling us who does and doesn't deserve positive or negative experiences?

For example: I used to say things like, "I didn't deserve to lose my daughter". This statement was meant to soothe my loss, however I noticed it actually triggered increasing sadness and pain within me. I saw losing my daughter as punishment and kept checking if I "deserved" the loss. This thought process was torturous.

Over time, I decided to explore more supportive ways to rephrase this for myself. I searched the vulnerability I was feeling and figured out that when I said, "I didn't deserve to lose a child", it indicated I valued connection and preferred to honour Eden's life. I felt like I was a mum, but didn't know how to express it because my child was no longer physically with me. I noticed that by creating an "I choose" statement, I increased my feeling of worth and my chances of living more peacefully, whilst respecting my loss.

Example above rephrased: "In light of my loss, *I choose* to value Eden's short life and myself as her mum". This feeling of worth helps to direct my feelings, thoughts and actions to increase an extra sense of purpose in my life.

Re-phrasing "I deserve" into an "I choose" statement enabled me to honour my love, whilst supporting my values for peace and connection. This empowered me to do volunteer work for the Mercy hospital, where I lost Eden and had Eloise. Re-directing my grief in a positive way through helping others gave me the opportunity to express my story and helped transform pain into strength.

Another bonus of moving away from "I deserve" is that I stopped asking "Why?". "Why?" is a very powerful question. However, in some situations it can throw us into the victim role. Questions like "Why me?" can leave us feeling trapped or punished. In some situations, there is no answer good enough.

For example: I realised there was no answers that would soothe my suffering, so I stopped asking "Why?" As a result, I found the energy to accept the situation and ask myself, "What can I do in light of this situation?"

Attempting to balance good and bad equally can be exhausting at times as our world is capable of moving and flowing without rhyme, reason or logic. When we stop looking for *fair outcomes*, it gives us more energy to find clarity within ourselves and explore other supportive choices. Increasing awareness of our needs and values is a far healthier strategy than trying to balance good and bad, or searching for whether or not we deserve to suffer. It's liberating to skip this unnecessary heartache.

For example: One day I got up early to attend to Eloise whilst my husband slept in. The next day I was too tired to get up. I heard my judging thoughts, *He should get up because I got up early yesterday!* – I was looking for fair. Before reacting with my autopilot, I paused to check in with how my body was feeling and yes I was tired. I rephrased my thought – *I value my health and choose to listen to what my body needs.* When Eloise asked me to get up, I merely said to my husband, "Will you take Eloise down stairs, I need more sleep. Thank you".

Although the thought process doesn't seem too different, there was no pressure from my internal voice to persuade my husband with "I deserve extra sleep", just the desire to give my body what it needed. He could hear my need minus the judgment, which increased my chances of getting his support, which I got – hooray for me!

I wish I could say I am always capable of this type of harmonious communication, but the truth is, when I don't pause and check in, my autopilot kicks in and the results are chaos.

Task To Support Choices

Write a statement that begins with "I deserve" (e.g. I deserve respect).

_____

_____

_____

_____

_____

_____

_____

Answering the following questions will firstly assist us to let go of the judgment underlining the feelings that arise from the above statement, and secondly, will help prepare us to build the "five to one" ratio as we aim to balance out our thought process and develop a "joyful amygdala".

What do I really need at this moment? (e.g. I need to feel connected, to be heard, loved.)

_____

_____

_____

_____

_____

What do I value most in this situation? (e.g. I value respect and kindness.)

_____

_____

_____

_____

_____

Chapter 2

In light of my need for ... I value ... I choose to ... (e.g. In light of my need to feel connected, I value respect, and hence I choose to spend more time with people who are considerate.)

A Mindful Moment: Just As I Am

I find a place to relax
Let my shoulders drop
I sit with respect
Accepting this moment just as it is

I focus on the rhythm of my breath
Notice the quality of my thoughts
As I make space for all thoughts
To come and go

At this moment, I embrace the things I like best about myself
And I accept the things I like not so much …
At this moment, I embrace the things I am great at
And I accept the things I am not so great at …

Checking in on my thoughts
I welcome any emotions that show up
Breathing in, and out, as I accept myself just as I am
In light of any feelings that arise

I choose to accept myself totally
I choose to be safe and healthy
I choose to be caring and respectful of myself
Just as I am

When ready,
I slowly bring my attention back to my surroundings
Bringing a sense of acceptance with me
As I move forward into my day.

Chapter 3

Concept: Sharing Experiences Harmoniously

Image courtesy of Luke Purchase and Irene Cornerstone (12 Moons Today).

> "... we do have a few clues that illuminate the relationship between the brain, our thoughts and the ability to communicate effectively. For example, everyday consciousness seems to be dependent on an area of the frontal lobes where short-term 'working memory' is processed. Our brain stores a tremendous amount of information in long-term memory, but when we carry out a task it must select only the pieces of information that relate to that task in a meaningful and appropriate way."
>
> - Andrew Newberg, M.D, and Mark Robert Waldman -

It is important to note that our brain is not a tape recorder or video camera. Our brain takes what it thinks is the most important information from an experience, relates this to past experiences and possible future experiences, so we can make informed choices. Hence, memory is a reconstruction of everything we experience. This is why there may be a group of people who witness one event and may all have varying opinions about what actually happened.

The way we use language also affects our experiences and the type of stories we tell ourselves. Often stories that have a hero, a victim and an antagonist are based on limited perspectives.

For example: "I like the dishes done after dinner every night and my husband doesn't want to help me do them." This story could be perceived as:

    a. I am the victim and he is the antagonist.
    b. He is the victim and I am the bully.
    c. I do the dishes and I am the hero.

Example above rephrased: "I prefer the dishes to be done after dinner and my husband is happy to do them the next day."

Mutual respect is evident in the rephrased statement; after all, feeling connected with my husband is more important to me than dishes. Noticing these drama roles can instantly empower our ability to identify our needs more readily. Putting forward the intention to connect with our values rather than focusing on a pre-conceived outcome, can lead to far more insightful resolutions.

For example: "After I lost my daughter I was so devastated that there were days I couldn't imagine how I could continue living. I didn't know how to live amongst all the families who had living children. No one seemed to understand me. It felt like people who hadn't lost a child could never know my real pain, so I would shut them out or I could not cope. I preferred to hang out with people who understood and acknowledged my pain." This story could be perceived as:

a. I am a "victim"
b. The people who don't understand are "antagonists".
c. Those who acknowledge my pain are "heroes".

Example above rephrased: "I am able to surf the positive and negative emotions that arise when reflecting on losing my daughter. I appreciate those that are able to acknowledge my experience, and understand that not everyone needs to comprehend my pain. I can accept compassion and I can be compassionate."

By noticing the roles and shifting my language, I created an opening for new pathways. My intention is to connect with my real needs and values as I explore ways to reflect on my experience and form healthy connections with others.

> "Everything we hear is an opinion, not fact.
> Everything we see is a perspective, not truth."
>
> - Marcus Aurelius -

Acknowledging we all have our own version of truth helps us become more open to each other's views; this encourages and attracts mutual connection. The drama roles are an ineffective way to deal with unresolved pain. Our language is more effective when our intention is to connect, interact and give each other space to be accountable. Sometimes we may need to give ourselves time in order to heal, grow and adapt our thoughts and actions, before deciding when and if we feel strong enough to move forward.

It is important to treat ourselves the way we would like others to treat us. Listening with compassion and respect helps us discover how others would like to be treated. To empower our connections, we can focus on listening with the purpose of hearing experiences, needs and values.

Language Shift: Get Specific

> "Success in life means living by your values."
>
> - Russ Harris -

Having preconceived ideals of how things "should be" can often hide the real problem in plain sight. The "should's", "ought to", "have to" type thinking gets us caught up in the past or worrying about the future.

For example: "It is 10.45pm, I should be in bed instead of working" translates to, "I'm wrong for being up and no matter what happens I can't make things right". Shifting this language to, "I'm tired and value my health. I would prefer to be sleeping so I will get this work done another time and go to bed," reveals my core issue. It enables me to connect with my values and find a comfortable resolution.

Focusing exclusively on "right and wrong" type thinking can prevent us from discovering what is really going on.

For example: "It's wrong for me to let my daughter watch too much television" simply translates to, "I prefer to have quality time with my daughter". I understand that there are some circumstances where "right and wrong" type thinking is needed, however if we get too caught up in this, we risk loosing an opportunity of finding more effective thought patterns.

For example: If I fixate on the thought "It's wrong for my daughter to watch too much television", then I can get drawn into the "what, why and how television affects our children", or I can simply choose to spend more quality time with my daughter. "Right and wrong" type thinking can create attachments to expectations, comparing to ideals and judging without acknowledging. "Right or wrong" is such a broad and complex concept when we consider all our unique qualities, cultures and different living environments.

To evolve out of unwarranted suffering and create healthier connections, we can approach this concept by being more specific. Notice how our thoughts and actions affect us. Are they:

- Healthy?
- Helpful?
- Comfortable?
- Supporting our values?
- Enhancing chances of fulfilling needs or not?

Focusing on increasing our awareness can guide us to live by our values. This is far more empowering than constantly trying to find "right and wrong".

Responding with awareness will help us become accountable for our own actions and facilitate us to be less dependent on having the outside world meet our needs. Being accountable enables us to develop connections towards authentic pathways and more equipped to live by our values.

> "He who lives in harmony with himself
> lives in harmony with the universe."
>
> - Marcus Aurelius -

Task To Support Being Specific

Write down one experience that has caused you pain, suffering or discomfort. To begin, ensure the pain is something small that you feel you can deal with. Then answer the questions below to re-set connection with your values. The length of these steps increases our chances of creating space between our thoughts and responses – a mindful moment to connect with our true needs.

Observe and write reactive dialogue. Be specific. Listen for judgment in our dialogue (e.g. I stub my toe and hear thought, "I am hopeless").

_____

_____

_____

What's beyond your thoughts? Listen for emotional and physical discomfort, or "indicators of needs" (e.g. "My body feels sore, tired and frustrated. I need to rest").

_____

_____

_____

What is happening here? (e.g. "My mind is elsewhere; I need to guide myself to the present moment").

_____

_____

_____

What do I value most in this situation? (e.g. "I value kindness and self-care").

_____

_____

_____

Re-phase experience (e.g. "That hurt, I am going to slow down and take better care of myself").

_____

_____

_____

A Mindful Moment: Inviting New Pathways

Find a comfortable position
To be calm for a moment
My spine supports me
As I focus on the natural flow of my breath

I imagine two doors creating space for me to pause
The first door closes me off from all past events
The second closes me off from any future events
In this space, I create a moment to get clear

For this moment
I become the observer of my mind
I scan my body for comfort and discomfort
Adjusting as needed to relax as best I can

I notice my emotions
Accepting both the comfortable and uncomfortable
As they communicate my current state
I explore any insights that arise

Breathing in, and out,
As I heal, adapt, and grow
I invite clarity
And am open to new pathways

Pause
Check in
Open the doors to clear
And supportive perspectives.

Chapter 4

Concept: Embracing Comfort And Discomfort

Image courtesy of Luke Purchase and Irene Cornerstone (12 Moons Today).

> "When you become comfortable with uncertainty, infinite possibilities open up in your life."
>
> - Eckhart Tolle -

Comfortable can be a cozy feeling, and yet it can also mean just feeling okay. Either way, being comfortable with uncertainty is often challenging. We love to know exactly what is going to happen and spend our lives trying to predict what will happen next.

Whilst watching movies, I often find myself calling out what I think is going to happen next. As I read stories to students, at times they can't help calling out predictions before I can finish a sentence. This is how we are wired – look into the past, and speculate what could happen, so we know how to react now. How do we adapt this approach to obtain the infinite possibilities Eckhart Tolle talks about? This question enticed me to take a deeper look.

One factor that influences our need for absolutes is "right and wrong" type thinking; it can create a false sense of perceived comfort. If we hear words like "They should", "I always", "He never", "They have to", or "We must", this indicates that we believe there is one correct path, and this can distract us from exploring more effective resolutions. When we hear statements similar to this, it frequently indicates that there is pain or discomfort that needs attending to.

For example: If I say, "They will never understand me", it translates to, "I feel hurt and would like others to understand me". Translating our pain directs us to the core of the issue so we can deal with it head on and skip any unwanted suffering.

Facing our pain with compassion supports us to transform adversities into strengths.

This requires:

- Acceptance
- Becoming aware of our inner-dialogue
- The ability to face our pain and vulnerabilities
- Developing our skills in setting clear boundaries
- The courage to seek support if the challenges are too great
- The willingness to try different approaches until we find what works.

Our thoughts have the ability to shape our reality; hence it makes sense to consider changing our thought patterns so we can move towards our preferred life experiences. Although it is much easier to relax in automatic thoughts, it also means we risk facing the same problems over and over, sometimes in new situations.

For example: Janet changed jobs every time she faced conflict. She was the "go-to person" when people needed help and she never seemed to get her work done on time. Janet decided to get some help from a coach and discovered she had been enabling this behaviour, so she set some boundaries. She created clear "no interruption times" and noted other times where she could be available to help people. People learned to wait or rearranged their time if they needed her, or asked others for help.

Becoming aware of our inner-dialogue helps us discover our "absolute-type thinking" and opens new avenues to navigate preferred pathways.

For example: When we hear dialogue such as, "This always happens", "I can't cope", "It's always like this", or

"There is no way", we can create a moment to breath and acknowledge our discomfort with compassion.

Being kind to ourselves under all circumstances is an important component before we can shift our language. This will invite a clear space between our thoughts and us, increasing our awareness as we explore how to transform discomfort into strengths.

> *"Change is the only constant."*
>
> *- Heraclitus -*

By shifting our internal dialogue to match our ever-changing lives, we increase our chances of finding opportunities towards inner-harmony.

Examples of how we could adapt these types of statements:

- "This always happens" – "This is uncomfortable, I need a new strategy".
- "I can't cope" – "This situation needs to change, I am open to alternatives".
- "That never works" – "This could be better, let's look for other possibilities".
- "There's no other way" – "I would prefer another option; I'll keep looking for other ways".

> *"Whatever you fight, you strengthen, and what you resist, persists."*
>
> *- Eckhart Tolle -*

Chapter 4

Acceptance is key to minimising our suffering. Facing our vulnerabilities can help us understand our real needs and values:

- *Look beyond our automatic responses* to discover our true needs by asking ourselves questions like, "Do I feel heard? Safe? Comfortable? Authentic? Understood? Acknowledged? Does this situation feel healthy? Do we feel trust or trusted?"
- *Become comfortable with the uncomfortable.* Rather than fighting or trying to erase discomfort, accept the discomfort as nature's communication method. Acceptance is different from condoning; acceptance acknowledges the situation for what it is and opens the door to freeing yourself from old pain.

Through acceptance and compassion we can create space to:

- Heal
- Grow
- Try new strategies
- Increase our perspectives
- Improve our ability to protect ourselves.

"When we learn to acknowledge, embrace and understand our suffering, we suffer much less. Not only that, but we're also able to go further and transform our suffering into understanding, compassion, joy for ourselves and for others."

- Thich Nhat Hanh -

Through sharing my experience I have noticed that hiding and avoiding suffering often leads to getting sick or becoming bitter. Since I've embraced my experiences in light of the pain, I am more able to explore healthier ways to express myself and live more harmoniously. This observation inspired me to face suffering with the intention to heal, grow and transform these experiences into strengths.

Language Shift: What's Happening Here?

One of my inspirational friends, Jacqui, prompted me to make this shift in a conversation about self-deprecating statements. I became aware of how unhelpful it is to ask questions like "What's wrong with me?" It tends to leave me feeling helpless. When I rephrased this to "What's happening here?" I felt invited to check in with myself. This assists me with most of my self-judging language. It helps me discover what my real needs are, and how to attend to them.

Isolating a situation from the past or potential future increases clarity. At times we can get tangled in a web of reactions based on past experiences. We cannot do anything about the past, so if we are experiencing a similar situation, we need to pay closer attention to notice what we may be missing in this moment.

For example: Jane's partner, Tom, felt that Jane started an argument every time he went out. He thinks she does this on purpose. He speaks to her in a defensive mode saying, "I'm going out now, any issues before I go?" Jane hears his tone as cold and aggressive. She thinks he is saying she has issues and that he can't wait to be away from her. This leads to the fight he was waiting for. Both of them feel rejected and unloved as a result. Jane noticed this pattern and started to change her perspective. The next time he was going out, she asked herself, *What's happening here?* She acknowledged that she was worthy of love under all circumstances. She knew Tom loved her, so she was willing to listen carefully. She noticed pain in Tom's face and realised he was actually trying to be caring, however his strategy was very confusing. The next time he asked a similar question, she tested out her theory and answered with, "Are you trying to say you would like an extra big hug before you go?" This snapped Tom out of his connection to past experiences and made him smile, resulting in a loving hug and no fight before he went out; a win-win for both parties.

To support us uncovering "What's really happening?" I would like to create an opening for mutual care and respect. To do this we need to become more aware of others and ourselves through:

- *Self care and respect.* Bringing suffering from the past or predicting future suffering into our present moment can heavily cloud our perspective. For example: A friend once said to me, "My new boyfriend yells at me all the time and I told him I already put up with my dad yelling at me when I was younger, I am no longer putting up with it". I reflected on what she said and responded, "Even if your dad didn't yell at you when you were younger, would it be okay for anyone to yell at you?" She responded, "No, I suppose not". So I asked, "Isn't it enough to say, I don't like being yelled at? I don't think you need to bring your past suffering into todays suffering to make a case". When we care and respect ourselves, we can give ourselves compassion, acknowledge our discomfort and give ourselves space to heal and grow.
- *Equal respect for others.* When we take on the perspective "We are all doing the best we can", we can hear beyond words and into the needs and values that underline thoughts and

actions. For example: If someone is yelling at us, they most likely don't feel heard. Yelling back will not help them feel heard, and they will be less likely to listen to us if they do not feel heard. We can know this and still yell back because it is human nature to protect ourselves. It takes many mindful moments to retrain ourselves to do this less often.

I encourage taking regular moments to check in with ourselves as a means to help discover and support our needs. If we do not feel safe, it is probably better to remove ourselves from a situation for a time. When we understand others, and place our ideas on an equal status with other people, we are more likely to be heard. More importantly, we can gain an extra perspective on what's really happening.

> "When you realise that no one really knows what they are doing and everyone is doing the best they can according to their own level of consciousness, life gets a lot easier."
>
> - Carl Sagan -

Task To Discover What Is Happening

Write down an unhelpful statement that you have heard yourself say. Reflect on the statement, notice any needs and values behind the unhelpful statement. Then follow the steps below to help gain a new understanding from the experience.

For example: Belinda scratched her car whilst parking.

- *Unhelpful thoughts:* "Nothing is going right for me, everything is going wrong."

- *What's happening here?* She felt disappointed and worried. She was pre-empting costs, predicting future complications and making lists about everything in her life that never went as planned, plus the pressure of being a single parent.
- *Let go of unhelpful thoughts.* She noticed her unhelpful thoughts rise, acknowledged that although those thoughts were efforts to support her, she could try a new strategy.
- *Needs/Values:* Belinda focused on her values; love for her daughter, safety and security.
- *Comfort and self-support:* She had compassion for herself and the discomfort she was feeling; "This is unfortunate, I am doing the best I can". She created time to plan and budget. She chose to have a garage sale and take on a little overtime at work to help her regain the feeling of security for her and her daughter.

Unhelpful thoughts:

_____

_____

_____

What is happening here? Reflection:

_____

_____

_____

Let go of unhelpful thoughts:

Needs and values:

Comfort and self-support:

Chapter 4

A Mindful Moment: Noticing What's Happening

*Find a comfortable place
I allow the earth to support me
I give my body permission to relax
And sit tall with pride*

*I notice how I am feeling at this moment
When an uncomfortable feeling comes up
I notice where the uncomfortable feeling is
Give this feeling my compassionate attention*

*As I notice my breath
I imagine the air going around
And through the discomfort
Creating space around it*

*I notice the parts of me that are comfortable
And create space
For both
The uncomfortable and comfortable to co-exist*

*When ready,
I slowly bring my attention back to my surroundings
I welcome awareness to be my loyal companion
As I re-enter my daily life.*

Chapter 5

Concept: Exploring Compassion

Image courtesy of Luke Purchase and Irene Cornerstone (12 Moons Today).

> "Any negative thought or feeling you have interferes with the parts of your brain that are involved with language processing, listening and speech."
>
> - Andrew Newberg, M.D., and Mark Robert Waldman -

One of my favourite stories from my role as a primary teacher was a time I attempted to help a student who was crying outside his classroom door. It was recess and I had just started yard duty. I felt heartbroken when I saw a prep boy, Jack, crying; his big eyes filled with tears. I approached Jack and asked, "Why are you crying?" He said that his friend Robert wouldn't play with him, so I set out to find Robert who was busy running away from him. When I finally caught up with Robert, I asked, "Why won't you play with Jack?" He replied with fear in his voice, "JJJJ-Jack has been throwing rocks at me". I turned to Jack and asked, "Why were you throwing rocks at Robert?" I was astounded when he replied, "Because he wouldn't play with me". I became curious about Jack's understanding of how his communication might affect others, so I asked him, "Did it work?" Jack looked at me with his big eyes, as his little hands indicated "so, so", as he said, "Not really".

I always thought Jack's response was so cute and naïve. However, later I found myself revisiting this story and questioning how my own communication strategies affect others. For example:

- When I am driving and someone cuts me off, I beep my horn and shake my fist because I would like others to be more considerate. Is it working? "Not really."

- When I would appreciate help with the housework and I call out, "You never help me with the housework!" Is it working? "Not really."
- I drop something and say to myself, "What's wrong with you? You're always dropping things". Is it working? "Not really."

I saw this type of communication happening around me constantly and wondered if there were more effective ways of acquiring and promoting understanding and compassion. Here are three alternative and healthier ways I could deal with the above scenarios:

1. When someone cuts me off in traffic, I could express my anger by yelling, "That is so frustrating, I feel so angry". This way, I am releasing the anger without creating the extra rage involved in attacking others and trying to control the way others are driving. This conserves my energy for more valuable tasks, like moving away from any danger. This way, no matter what happens, I have expressed my emotion in a healthy way, and supported my need to be safe.
2. Rather than say, "You never help me with the housework", I could say, "I am aiming to get the house cleaned this weekend, would you prefer doing the vacuuming, or hanging up clothes?" Making a request will be a clearer message than attacking someone based on fear of not getting help.
3. When I drop something, I could check, "How am I feeling? Am I tired or trying to do too much? What could I do to support the way I would prefer to feel?" This might mean I stop what I am doing and re-prioritise to better suit the situation I am in at the time.

I am so thankful for my student's innocent "so, so" hand gesture with the "Not really!" comment. Whenever things are not in line with the way I hope, I ask myself, "Is it working?" If the answer is "Not really!" I have an opportunity to check in and adapt my behaviour in order to match my true needs and values.

I have often heard people say, myself included, "I shouldn't complain, there are others out there with worse problems". Although this is a reasonable statement, it is healthier to create a safe space to express our emotions clearly than to try to squash them.

For example: "I understand things could be worse, however it would be healthier to change the way I approach housework to prevent burn-out." Rephrasing this statement addresses our real concern, gives us a healthy dose of self-compassion and opens our perspective towards finding better ways of caring for ourselves, whilst we consider a respectful way to recruit help.

Our emotions indicate whether or not our basic human needs are met; dealing with each situation authentically helps us develop more caring connections. When we can respect our emotions whilst respecting other people's emotions, we strengthen our character and the way we communicate with others and ourselves.

If I look at life using only my current knowledge, history and perceptions, I imagine everyone sees the world how I do, and start wondering why everyone isn't "behaving correctly". However, when I accept that each of us brings varied knowledge, history and views to each situation, I increase my perspective and the quality of my ability to relate to others and myself.

Compassion helps us to feel cared for, understood and appreciated. We can give compassion, even when we totally disagree with each other. It is the ability to have equal compassion for yourself and others that invites a more peaceful existence.

For example: Whilst at work, Sarah sent Vivian seven long text messages back-to-back. Although this made Vivian uncomfortable, she could sense Sarah needed to feel heard. She took a moment to acknowledge herself and considered how Sarah might be feeling. Vivian sent one message, "I understand you need to talk. At the same time I am at work. Are you available to talk after 7pm so I can give you all my attention?"

Acquiring and promoting compassion requires us to take a moment to check in on how we feel. When listening carefully to our own discomfort, we feel heard and acquire a sense of self-acceptance. Knowing we are worthy of safety, love and respect under all circumstances, gives us the inner-strength to check for alternative ways to deal with each situation as they arise.

Language Shift: Expand our Perspectives

> "All violent actions and behaviours are
> a tragic expression of our unmet needs."
>
> - Marshall Rosenberg -

I see most conflicts as an opportunity to develop a better understanding of each other and improve our connection. Yes, being challenged is uncomfortable, however I prefer to grow than to stay static.

Often when faced with conflict we take a "black and white" type thinking approach or an "all or nothing" attitude; this is when our emotions go to the extremes and there is no middle ground. To expand and deepen our perspective, we can interpret our emotions to notice what needs have or haven't been met.

Noticing our "good" feelings indicates that our needs are met. Do we feel:

- Safe?
- Trusted?
- Understood?
- Comfortable?
- Accepted?

Noticing our "bad" feelings indicates un-met needs. Do we feel:

- Misunderstood?
- Unappreciated?
- Lonely?
- Awkward?
- Misjudged?

It is important to note that "bad" feelings often need time to calm before we are aware of our true needs and values.

For example: "I am angry with Monique for canceling our catch up". When I take a moment to check in, I notice I am not angry with Monique; I feel angry because I have had a challenging day and was looking forward to her company. I notice that although I am disappointed our catch up was cancelled, I am able to create a calm space to recover from my challenging day in other ways.

Rather than classifying ourselves as "good" or "bad", it would be more effective to notice the underlying needs of the good and the bad feelings.

For example: "I am angry about a misunderstanding with Brie, at the same time I am grateful for the mutual respect we have for each other. I value our friendship so when I calm down, I am able to call her and focus on listening and speaking with extra compassion."

Labeling and judging can make us feel threatened. Taking away the labels and judgment helps our internal world stay calm and connected to our whole brain, increasing our capacity to resolve situations with greater consideration.

Replacing this pattern of judging with compassion and a deeper understanding of what we need, can transform the way we communicate with each other.

Task Promoting Expanding our Perspectives

This task is inspired by Dr. Rick Hanson's "five to one" ratio.

Write about something that has caused you discomfort.

For example: Driving to and from work can often make me feel uncomfortable. This morning as I drove to work, I came to my first red light and thought, "I wish this light was green so I could hurry up and get to work".

_____

_____

_____

_____

Notice any "uncomfortable" feelings that arise. At the same time, explore any helpful and comfortable feelings or behaviours that could support positive thoughts and feelings in light of this experience, and write five down below. Take "20 to 30 seconds" to enjoy any positive emotions you have noticed.

For example: This morning whilst at the stoplight, I created the opportunity to notice and appreciate five positive experiences:

1. Took some deep breaths
2. Listened to sounds around me; other cars, the wind and the birds in the trees
3. Noticed the sky; it had a beautiful pink tinge behind the dark blue/grey clouds, with a hint of clear sky in the background
4. Smiled at my daughter in the back seat who was looking at a book
5. Felt a moment of peace and stillness before moving with the traffic.

Positive Moments

1.
2.
3.
4.
5.

A Mindful Moment: Cultivating Compassion

Note: This meditation revisits and extends our practice of accepting ourselves and accepting others.

Begin by sitting comfortably
I allow my feet to connect to the floor
As my breath flows naturally
In and out of my body

At this moment, I embrace the things I like best about myself,
With compassion, I accept the things I like not so much
I embrace the things I am great at
And accept the things I am not so great at

Breathing in, and out,
I choose to accept myself just as I am

I now bring to mind someone I would like to increase understanding with
For this moment, I embrace the things I like best about them,
And with compassion, I accept the things I like not so much
I embrace the things they are great at
And I accept the things they are not so great at

With compassion,
I acknowledge my feelings and thoughts
Respecting others just as they are
With equal respect for myself

I allow a sense of ease to surround me
Freedom for all of us to be just as we are
And space for us to connect and grow

When ready,
I slowly bring my attention back to my surroundings
Inviting compassion to join me
As I re-enter my daily life.

Chapter 6

Concept: Beyond Thoughts

Image courtesy of Luke Purchase and Irene Cornerstone (12 Moons Today).

> "Don't take your thoughts too seriously."
> - Eckhart Tolle -

Getting attached to thoughts, labels, ideals or experiences can distract us from our real needs in the present moment.

For example: I have heard myself say, "I am a teacher, so I should be a confident speller". By attaching to the label *teacher* and to my ideas of what I think teachers should be able to do, I am judging myself and creating "fixed ideals." This attachment can leave me feeling stuck.

By observing our thoughts, we can differentiate between who we think we are or should be, compared to our true authentic selves. This will support an increased healthy state of mind and help expand our opportunities.

Example above rephrased: "In my role as a teacher, I would enjoy being a confident speller." This statement helps me separate my role as a teacher from my authentic self, leading me to my true needs. It is also accepting of where I am at the moment, and opens opportunities for me to build my confidence and skills.

> "Observing without evaluating is the highest form of human intelligence."
> - J. Krishnamurti -

Observing ourselves minus evaluation can help us move away from fixating on old thoughts and experiences.

For example: When saying things like "I am angry", it is challenging to make a clear observation. Attaching to the word "angry" can cloud my perspective and prevent me from seeing a wider range of options that may be available. We can adjust our observational position by saying something like "At this moment, I am experiencing anger". The space between "at the moment, I am experiencing" and "anger" makes way for noticing a moment of emotion minus any attachment and judgment. This allows for a mindful reflection enabling us to find calm and clarity.

For example: One day I was driving home with Eloise (she was a one-year-old at that time). Eloise was crying from the minute we got in the car; it was incredibly challenging and frustrating. I didn't know how to comfort her and, at the same time, I needed to stay focused on driving safely. Within myself I created an *internal buffer zone* to help me check in. I was able to accept:

- It is healthy for Eloise to express her frustration.
- I needed equal quality empathy for her discomfort and mine.
- My irritated feelings were a reflection of my love and desire to keep us safe.
- A conscious choice to focus on the road would support my value for safety.
- Taking conscious deep breaths would help my brain and body stay calm.

For me to listen beyond my thoughts, I needed to first accept the situation as it was and allow the discomfort to be there. Because I had been practicing mindful moments daily, I was able to maintain a sense of calm and focused on observing without judging. Eloise's crying eventually appeared to ease and my ability to focus on driving us home safely was achieved.

Although this process takes longer than my automatic reactions, in the long term, it has better supported my wellbeing. Over time, this new process has become more automatic for me and I don't need to work so hard to create the space between discomfort and my inner calm voice.

> *"Insanity is doing the same thing over and over again and expecting different results."*
>
> - Albert Einstein -

Our thoughts lead our behaviour. Thinking the same thoughts over and over will activate repetitive behaviours, leading to similar results, even in different circumstances. Being aware of this and introducing new pathways can help us interrupt self-sabotaging patterns.

For example: I experienced extreme discomfort with Eloise (around two-years-old at the time) refusing to cooperate with changing her nappy. My repetitive thought was, *She is always so difficult and doesn't stay still when it's time to change her nappy.* One day she got to the point of crying beyond control. I was so angry and frustrated, I found myself screaming, "ENOUGH!"

Next time I was in a similar situation, I took a few deep breaths and gave myself a moment to increase my perspective using compassion. The ability to do this is reinforced by practicing mindful moments daily. I thought about Eloise's need to feel a sense of independence; when I heard the beginning of the "I refuse to get my nappy changed" path, I asked her "What do we need to do? Would you like to get the mat? The wipes?" These questions derailed her protest and I avoided one big conflict. "Phew!" I was relieved.

The way we speak to others is an extension of the way we speak to ourselves. When I hear myself speak in an aggressive manner, I notice my thoughts are equally harmful. Aggressive conduct is a poor strategy when aiming for connection, love, peace and mutual respect. Becoming aware of real needs and values can often prevent the need for aggressive strategies.

When we focus on connecting and supporting a sense of harmony, we can find peaceful solutions in many more aspects of our lives. By listening beyond thoughts we can discover what each situation really needs.

Language Shift: What Am I Willing To Do?

"I should"-type statements are pain hidden in plain sight. They lure us into judging or comparing to ideals from the past or possible future. This holds us back from seeing other perspectives and from connecting with our real needs.

For example: When I think to myself "I should have phoned my aunty to check on how she is going," I focus on the fact I haven't called her. If I notice my discomfort and rephrase this to, "I am disappointed that I didn't call my aunty yet", then I can easily focus on making another time to call her without causing myself extra suffering for not calling her.

To create a healthy space between self and thoughts, when we hear statements like "I should", we can ask our selves:

- "How am I feeling at this moment?"
- "How would I prefer to feel?"

OR

- "Do I feel safe at the moment?"
- "What can I do to increase my chances of being safe?"

When we explore beyond statements like "I should", we can shift our thinking to a more helpful position. We can discover what we are willing to do to increase our chances of finding comfort. This is when words like "could" or "I am willing to" can support our intentions to connect more harmoniously.

For example: "I should be able to have children like everyone else", translates to, "I am willing to increase my chances of having children. I am willing to try alternative options". This type of thinking supported me whilst I battled through an eight-year journey of loss and hope to become a mother.

We can use this method to rephrase when we hear any inner-dialogue that leaves us feeling stuck. Here are some examples of how we can open up to new options:

- "I have to go", translates to, "I am willing to go for one hour".
- "I must help", translates to, "When I have completed this task, I could be able to help".
- "I have no choice", translates to, "I would consider doing this another time".

Each statement creates time to check-in with ourselves and create boundaries. Caring for others and ourselves equally increases our chances of a peaceful existence. It is not "either or", it is "together we support each other's needs". Striving towards win-win resolutions (rather than win-lose) is how we can increase our opportunities for living a more harmonious existence.

Task To Support Values

Write down three statements starting with "I should" (e.g. "I should be more fit").

Notice what you value in these statements (e.g. "I value my health").

Notice what you are willing to let go of (e.g. "I need to let go of my past efforts and worries of failing so I can focus on my current self).

Rephrase your statements using words like "I am willing to", "I could", "I value", or "I intend" (e.g. "I am willing to accept myself just as I am. I intend to care for myself and make healthier choices, beginning with walking once a week", or "I am willing to treat myself with respect and intend to value my health, starting with eating more vegetables and drinking more water").

"I should" statement:

Values:

_____

_____

I am willing to:

_____

_____

I am willing to let go of:

_____

_____

"I should" statement:

_____
_____
_____

Values:

_____
_____
_____

I am willing to:

_____
_____
_____

I am willing to let go of:

_____
_____
_____

Chapter 6

"I should" statement:

_____

_____

_____

Values:

_____

_____

_____

I am willing to:

_____

_____

_____

I am willing to let go of:

_____

_____

_____

A Mindful Moment: Self-Respect

I find a quiet and comfortable place
To be still
I tune into my breath
Thoughts and feelings

Just for this moment,
I allow myself to feel free from all that has happened
Free from all that could ever happen
I take a break from life as it is

I notice the quality of my thoughts
And then bring my focus to a feeling of respect
With the intention
To support my wellbeing

I explore what respect means to me
How it feels and how it sounds
Acknowledging the genuine support
Respect can bring to my health

I allow respect to flow
In and around me
As it becomes my guide
And companion

Take a moment
To pause
Check-in
And re-set.

Chapter 7

Concept: Bringing New Light To Positive And Negative

Image courtesy of Luke Purchase and Irene Cornerstone (12 Moons Today).

> "Out beyond ideas of wrongdoing and rightdoing, there is a field. I'll meet you there."
>
> - Mevlana Jelaluddin Rumi -

Positive and negative thoughts can act like an "on and off" switch in our brain. However, if we envision them as part of a team, directing our attention to whether our values are met, we can bring new light to their purpose. If a situation feels right, it indicates we are meeting values (e.g. we feel safe, healthy and respected). If a situation feels wrong, our values are not being met (e.g. we do not feel completely safe, healthy or respected). By acknowledging our feelings and fueling self-care, we enhance our chances of being calm and improving our wellbeing.

For example: The statement, "I think it is wrong to stay up late the night before work", indicates that I value my health and my job. Rephrasing this statement to, "I value my sleep, especially the night before work" is non-judgmental and will not add extra suffering if for some reason I do not get an early night sleep.

When we are curious about the values we hold, and those of others, we are more able to address challenges, as they arise. Questions towards forming peaceful dialogue may be "Would I prefer to":

- Control what is happening, or be open to growth?
- Attach to what people say, or be objective and open to other perspectives?
- Predict to within an inch of my life, or build my instincts?

- Hold onto idealistic views, or connect on the level of needs and values?

Our internal world can be calmer when we are more aware of our values. It's important to note that having the intention to connect may mean that outcomes are different to what we expect. This sense of mutual respect and sharing responsibility is essential towards creating a peaceful existence.

> "If we ask two questions, we will see that punishment never works.
> First: What do we want the other person to do?
> Second: What do we want the other person's reasons to be for doing as we request?"
>
> - Marshall Rosenberg -

Reward and punishment appear to be a quick strategy to help direct behaviour. However, it is not always the best approach for long-lasting resolutions.

For example: I may choose to take on a fitness routine to change my body shape. Rewarding myself with a new outfit may motivate me to stay fit for a short time; this is external motivation. If I do not follow the routine, I may feel upset and then punish myself as a means of motivation.

Unfortunately, this will leave me feeling worse than I already feel. However, if I focus on my value to stay healthy, I can make informed choices moment-to-moment; this is internal motivation. It might take longer than punishment, but it will lead to healthier results.

Punishment will intensify our emotions and can trigger our amygdala, which switches off our more considered and logical thought processes. Losing our rational mind is not optimal if we are trying to discover the best ways to stay healthy and safe.

For example: If I say to myself, "I am useless, I should have gone for a walk instead of sleeping in", I am judging and punishing myself. This will further inflame my emotions, which will most likely lead to unhealthy thought patterns and behaviours. However, if I can hear the discomfort and pain beyond my words, I can find self-compassion and prepare myself to adapt to a more supportive inner-dialogue to better support my wellbeing.

I could respond with, "I didn't enjoy the results of sleeping in, I am going to take a different approach tomorrow. I will prepare for bed an hour earlier to ensure I get enough rest. I will call a friend and set up a *walk-and-talk* catch up to motivate me to stay on track". This acknowledges my feelings whilst being open to new opportunities, re-directing my behaviour without unnecessary harm.

Noticing our feelings and thought patterns can help us clearly portray which direction to take.

For example: Saying "Get out" to someone can further aggravate a situation. However, saying, "I need some time to process this" is a clear boundary indicating you will consider the situation from both sides. You are respecting others and your needs equally.

Taking a mindful moment to support our values can also help us acknowledge regrets and create an opening towards mutual respect. By redirecting our thoughts, we enable preferred actions and a clearer direction; being transparent about regrets empowers our harmonious intentions.

Chapter 7

"Our survival as a species depends on our ability to recognise that our wellbeing and the wellbeing of others are in fact one and the same."

- Marshall Rosenberg -

Trust and respect grow when both parties feel heard, understood and are supportive of each other's needs. This is where win-win thinking patterns can re-direct our choices towards respectful connections.

The word "sorry" is sometimes used like a Band-Aid towards making peace with ourselves or others. "Sorry" doesn't always settle a problem or help us build a deeper understanding of each other's needs. It would be clearer and more helpful to say something like:

- I regret what happened and I will do my best to ensure it doesn't happen again.
- I acknowledge that my actions hurt you, let's plan a different approach for these situations.
- I hear your pain and will consider your feelings and thoughts on this matter.
- I understand you more now and have an increased awareness with this new perspective.

If we feel "right" or "wrong", we may change our actions to suit each other accordingly and then feel resentment. If we acknowledge and consider each other equally, there is a chance for stronger connection; this may also give us extra insight to our current views.

Before we can shift our language, we need to check our values.

For example: I value safety. When I rush to get ready for work and leave my phone at home, I do not feel so safe. It's not so much about leaving my phone at home, as it is about being able to trust myself to stay safe.

Create a PLACE for peace to grow:

    Pause and reflect (e.g. at this moment I feel frustrated)

    Listen for values (e.g. I value respect and safety)

    Accept (e.g. I am doing the best I can to be safe and to respect myself)

    Check what is needed (e.g. a moment to check I have everything before I leave)

    Extra care (e.g. be extra caring to self under all circumstances).

When we make a habit of checking-in, especially during rough patches, we teach ourselves how to adapt and build trust in ourselves.

Building self-trust is an incredibly rewarding and empowering practice. When we can trust ourselves, we feel more secure and confident to interact on a mutually respectful basis.

> "... Become the change we wish to see in the world."
> - Mahatma Ghandi -

Language Shift: Win-Win Thinking Patterns

Our emotions can feel torn when we are in conflict. It feels horrible to lose, and winning can be a short-lived experience, especially when our opponent is a loved one. At times conflict is inescapable, and most often, uncomfortable for all involved. Deep down we know that avoiding conflict or letting it build up can make things worse. However, if we shift our perspective and language, we can welcome conflict as an insightful tool towards helping us build stronger relationships.

> "Synergy is what happens when one plus one equals ten or a hundred or even a thousand! It's the profound result when two or more respectful human beings determine to go beyond their preconceived ideas to meet a great challenge."
>
> - Stephen Covey -

By evolving past our preconceived ideas to meet challenges, we can create win-win resolutions. This requires a high level of acceptance, self-awareness and measured vulnerability, as well as being open to other perspectives.

Practicing acceptance and vulnerability can feel weak to start off with; it may feel a bit like we have given up or given in. However, this practice strengthens us mentally and emotionally as it encourages us to face any issues we may have head on.

Being open to other perspectives and being able to share our perspectives clearly unlocks many opportunities to resolutions we may not have thought of. Our regular internal dialogue needs to reflect an intention to connect beyond our own perspective, so that we can be prepared in conflict situations.

When we are treated in a manner we dislike, we need to be willing to monitor our thoughts and behaviour, in order to discover how we are contributing to the way we are being treated. We may be giving others unclear or mixed messages that lead them to treat us poorly.

For example: Anthony, "Why did you put the kids toys in this room?" Maya reacts by defending her actions. His question is interrogating; he is searching for "right and wrong". By explaining herself, she deems this communication style as acceptable. Her defensive approach also adds fuel to his judging tone.

If Maya responded with a statement like, "So you are curious as to why the kids toys are in this room", she could quickly change the dynamics of the situation. Showing authentic interest in Anthony's question, minus the judgments, can derail his interrogation.

This would provide a safe atmosphere for them to slowly build a path towards mutual respect and connection. It could take Anthony a while to get used to her not playing the "right" verses "wrong" game. However, over time he would discover that she has strong respectful boundaries and will not participate in aggressive conversations.

When we behave accountably, we can clearly negotiate our interactions. By creating an intention to treat ourselves with respect and exploring resolutions that meet each other's needs, we empower our chances of building harmonious relationships.

Once we are in conflict, it can be very challenging to create harmonious communication. However, if we practice win-win thought patterns in calm times, we will increase our chances of finding the peaceful language needed when we encounter challenging scenarios.

It is important to practice words and phrases that provide a non-threatening place to build our connections. Statements to support win-win thinking patterns sound like:

- I hear you ... (rephrase what was said and check you understood) ... "I am not comfortable with that... I would prefer... "
- "I acknowledge your views ... My views differ from that ... How about we consider other options."
- "Once I have processed this information, I will get back to you."
- "I appreciate you need ... However, you will need to find someone else to help you with that."
- "I hear your suggestion ... At the same time I feel ... Would you consider ... "
- "I understand that from your perspective ... From my perspective ... Let's think about it so we can create a win-win situation here?"
- "I sense you're frustration and respect your response. Let's make another time to talk about this when we are both calm."
- "I am not comfortable with that suggestion. However, I am open to hearing other ideas."
- "At this stage, I am feeling uncomfortable. I will go for a walk to settle my thoughts and get back to you." (You may like to give a time frame e.g. five minutes or an hour.)

Task To Support Win-Win Thinking

These reflective questions are a guide; use the ones most relevant to your situation.

Challenging situation (e.g. People call and interrupt me whilst I am working from home).

_____

_____

_____

Check what values underline this issue (e.g. I value a balance between connections in my personal and professional life. I value the feeling of purpose and security I get from my work).

_____

_____

_____

Check for accuracy (e.g. Not everyone can see that I am working from home. I respect others and myself equally).

_____

_____

_____

Consider other viewpoints (e.g. I am grateful that I can work from home and that there are people who call me. People call to connect).

_____

_____

_____

Chapter 7

How does this affect you? Is it worth participating in this situation? (e.g. The calls distract me from completing my work on time. I need to complete my work without interruptions. I notice that I really enjoy talking to people more when I can give them my full attention).

_____

_____

_____

What are you willing to do in this situation? (e.g. Set clear boundaries to help set me up for success; divert my phone whilst working on important projects).

_____

_____

_____

What is a mutually respectful way you could respond? (e.g. Divert my phone to a message that asks, "When is a good time to call you back?" This creates a defined work time and I am able to note appropriate times to respond to people's messages).

_____

_____

_____

A Mindful Moment: Clarity

I find a moment to pause

Each breath puts extra space
Between me and the past
And each breath adds reflection time,
Before I move forward

I allow myself to feel free
As I reflect on my wellbeing
I notice my breath
And make space to get clear

I slowly breathe in, and out,
Observing and accepting any
Thoughts and feelings
That may surface

I check in on
My heart,
As I observe without judging
And make space for clarity

I take another moment
To notice my body
Scanning from head to toe
With compassion

In this space I can choose to
Feel free, safe and respected
As I welcome clearer perspectives
Into my daily life.

Chapter 8

Concept: Peaceful Connections

Image courtesy of Elizabeth Moran.

Peaceful connections begin with self-acceptance. When we accept and understand ourselves, we can develop strategies to set boundaries that help keep us safe and respected. This requires self-trust and knowing we will do our best to face whatever life dishes out.

Being able to accept ourselves grows from treating ourselves with care, regardless of whether or not we are at our best. To build self-trust and strength, it is important to appreciate ourselves no matter what happens. It is this unconditional kindness that results in healthier choices, as our efforts are not lost on extreme ups and downs.

Self-acceptance also helps us practice acknowledging where we are at, as a result of past events and thought patterns. Knowing this empowers us to check in with our internal world by asking questions like:

- How am I feeling at this moment?
- What do I really value in this situation?
- Do my actions match how I would prefer to feel?
- Can I adapt my thought patterns to support my needs and values?
- Could I modify my behaviour to match how I would like to feel?

If we keep doing today what suited us yesterday, we may keep getting into the same challenging situations. Something that matched our needs yesterday may not work for us today, so to evolve, we need to grow with ourselves. Our quest for peace is honoured through an ongoing daily practice of checking that our thoughts, attitudes, and actions are *up to date* with our current needs and values.

Chapter 8

> "Most people are afraid of suffering. But suffering is a kind of mud to help the lotus flower of happiness grow. There can be no lotus flower without the mud."
>
> - Thich Nhat Hanh -

Sometimes when we are suffering, we start to think of all the things that have ever hurt us. This can cloud our thoughts, making it more difficult to listen to our real needs. When we acknowledge the past and possible future outcomes as only thoughts, we increase our chances of discovering what is needed for healing, growth and transformation.

For example: When I hear myself make statements like, "Well, nothing ever works out for me", I always expect the worst. There is a false sense of power because if I am going to suffer, at least I had predicted it and therefore "I am right"?

When we hear these types of thoughts, we can ask questions like, "Do I feel safe and healthy? What can I do at this moment to feel safe and healthy?" Sometimes, just listening to ourselves is enough. Other times we may need to take action and express thoughts or emotions to help redirect relationship connections in our lives.

For example: One day I visited my parents, I was in a hurry and almost left without saying goodbye to my dad. He is often pottering around the house and I have spent many occasions chasing him down to say goodbye, so when I am in a hurry, I sometimes don't realise he is home.

On this occasion, I saw him and said, "Dad, I nearly forgot to say goodbye".

With an aggressive tone he said, "You always forget to say goodbye".

I was able to hear the hurt in his voice that underlined his response and I said, "So you feel like I often forget to say goodbye? I am sorry to hear that, I will make more effort in future".

Once he felt heard and considered, I didn't face that conflict again, especially since I now make more effort find him to say goodbye. I could have fought to be understood, but I know my intentions are loving and I am doing the best I can, so I didn't feel the need to prove myself "right or wrong".

> "The art of happiness is also the art of managing suffering."
> - Thich Nhat Hanh -

Suffering and happiness co-exist and are continually changing. Feelings are not static; they are constantly on the move, as are our thoughts and attitudes.

In Thich Nhat Hanh's book *No Mud, No Lotus*, he describes how the lotus flower wilts and becomes the compost for another lotus flower to grow; this is quite powerful in relation to how we can transform our pain and suffering into strengths. He explains how happiness "can become suffering and suffering can become happiness again"; happiness and suffering are organic and "impermanent by nature", hence becoming attached to either suffering or happiness is not helpful.

Imagine if, rather than making our lives into continuous stories of "good and bad", "victims, bullies and heroes" we just notice happiness, absorb and enjoy it. And observe our suffering, allowing it to pass, knowing with time, guidance and space, it will transform back into happiness.

Chapter 8

"We are a vast ocean of awareness, and even with a regular ocean, there could be a typhoon or hurricane on the surface, but you go 20 or 30 feet deep, and it's calm. The same thing is true with us.

On the surface, we could be going through an emotional hurricane, but if you go just a little deeper, you'll see this calmness, vastness, spaciousness that is really what's always here. It's just we lose touch with it when the turmoil is boiling on the surface."

- Hale Dwoskin -

Our inner-core is calm and peaceful; it is unaffected by anything that is going on in our lives. Our inner-core is sometimes likened to the sky, always calm and clear. And our feelings are like the weather; continuously on the move, just passing through, and covering up the calm background. Also like the weather, there may be some things in life we cannot change or control, however, we can make more regular healthy, respectful and well considered choices to steer ourselves towards preferred experiences.

When using our senses, we can anchor ourselves and create a mindful moment. Thoughts of past or future can add an extra layer of unnecessary suffering. Acceptance of our current situation is vital to finding hints of peace, as we connect to our centred calm.

"One conscious breath, in and out, is a meditation."

- Eckhart Tolle -

One of the most helpful ideas I found through Eckhart Tolle's work was that taking a conscious breath can support inner-peace. He suggested making a time in the day to take a few conscious breaths, like when you get in the car or when you are washing your hands. I have found that having a fragrant hand soap to wash my hands is one way to remind myself to take conscious breaths and check on how I am feeling.

By becoming aware of our senses, we increase our chances of creating conscious choices and behaving accountably for our actions. By improving this feeling of checking-in with self-care, openness and respect, it opens doors for us to live with the intention to support our wellbeing.

> "Vulnerability is the birthplace of love, belonging, joy, courage, empathy, and creativity. It is the source of hope, empathy, accountability, and authenticity. If we want greater clarity in our purpose or deeper and more meaningful spiritual lives, vulnerability is the path."
>
> - Brené Brown -

In Brené Brown's book *Daring Greatly*, she shares how her research on vulnerability opens up to opportunities of developing our inner-strength. When we understand others and ourselves more clearly, and choose to interact with authenticity, we can live with purpose and encourage a deeper connection.

Eckhart's wisdom in his book *The Power Of Now* highlights the importance of being present, accepting life moment by moment, and how to notice thoughts are just thoughts. Our ability to "be in the moment" empowers us to create a clearer mind, so that we enjoy life without constantly being dragged into the past or future.

Chapter 8

Brené Brown's book *The Power Of Vulnerability* is extraordinarily comforting and inspiring, as she exposes the need to lean into discomfort and embrace vulnerability. I love the way she refers to people who embrace vulnerability as the "Wholehearted"; to me, these people sound a lot like Dr Rick Hanson's reference to the people with a "joyful amygdala".

If we can blend Eckhart's *Power Of The Now*, Brené Brown's *Power Of Vulnerability*, and Rick Hanson's power of the "joyful amygdala", we can meet our needs more effectively.

Becoming aware of our breath throughout the day enables us to create mindful moments to reflect before choosing each new step. Taking a moment to breathe consciously when we feel vulnerable, can help us clear our minds and tap into our needs. For example:

- When I am getting ready for work and would like to ensure I have everything I need before leaving for work, I take a focused breath and create a moment to check-in.
- When I lock the house, I take a conscious breath and feel the action of locking the door, and note how it feels after it is locked.
- When I put items away, I take a focused breath as a way of feeling safe and increasing the chances that I will remember where I put them.

For us to discover peaceful connections we need to face our vulnerabilities; this requires self-acceptance. Each time we look in the mirror, we may tend to judge ourselves harshly. Looking at ourselves with acceptance, with the intention to be healthy, safe and respectful, builds self-trust and connection with our core-self. When we treat ourselves with compassion, treating others with the same level of respect becomes second nature. This is key to enabling peaceful connections.

Language Shift: Checking In

"Good luck" and "bad luck" are words that imply we are powerless. After I lost Eden, I told my grief therapist "I felt jinxed, because it seemed everyone but me was be able to have living babies" (please note this was my grieving perception at the time and my thoughts were driven by pain). Her response was simple: accept what is, do what you can to increase your chances of having a baby, and try to find moments where you can enjoy life as you go.

This "increase your chances" advice has been close to my heart ever since that day. I translate it to everything I do. I ask myself, *What would you like to do next? What can I do to increase my chances of achieving that? What don't I like? What can I do at this moment to decrease the likelihood of being unsafe?*

Sometimes there is something I can do. Other times, all I can do is accept what is and guide myself to ride the storm. The peaceful feeling that comes with this language reflects that I am doing everything I can to be safe, self-caring and aware.

Whenever we are having feelings that are uncomfortable, awkward or just make us feel unsure, rather than squashing these feelings, we can choose to respect them and listen to our senses by using our feelings as indicators.

When my daughter was learning to walk using a baby walking trolley, she would often crash into a wall and call out for help. I remember saying to her, "You need to change direction, then you can keep going".

This got me wondering if that simple statement would work in my life whenever I got stuck, and it does. Whenever something is not working, I think, *Time to adjust and change direction.*

Slowly adapting our internal reaction to stop and pause before choosing which actions to take, supports healthy and safe choices. When we are stuck or frustrated, we could notice our auto-reaction and check-in on how we are feeling, the quality of thoughts we are experiencing, our actions and on what is happening around us.

Task Supporting Checking In

In this moment, I notice (e.g. I notice I have 10 minutes before going out to dinner with my family).

_____

_____

_____

_____

What do I value most? (e.g. I value love for my family).

_____

_____

_____

_____

Which thoughts are helpful to my needs? (e.g. Focus on enjoying that I am ready to go).

_____

_____

_____

_____

How could I respect others? (e.g. Giving space to my husband and daughter to prepare in their own way).

How could I show myself respect? (e.g. Enjoy a few minutes of calm to myself before we leave).

How could I support my values? (e.g. Focus on staying safe and listening carefully to myself and those around me).

Chapter 8

A Mindful Moment: Peaceful Connections

In this moment
I find space to be still
As I pause and
Check-in

I notice the quality of my emotions
And look for any feelings of peace
As I breathe in, and out,
I check on my wellbeing

I bring to mind a feeling of calm
And notice how it feels
To bring a sense of peace
To this moment

I focus on
My heart, body and mind
As I embrace the feeling of harmony
Feel how peace can genuinely support my health

I set my intention
To notice opportunities to find peace
And allow this sense of harmony to become part of my
Attitude, thoughts and actions

I invite peace to be
Around and within me
As it becomes a guide
For my heart and mind

Take a moment to check-in
And breathe kindness in, and out, of my body
Being open to peaceful connections
I re-set and return to my surroundings.

Conclusion

Image courtesy of Jane Power.

This morning whilst getting ready to leave for work, I dropped my keys. As I picked them up, I heard a supportive inner-voice say, "It's going to be okay". I have a far away memory of an old inner-voice that would have cursed me and said things like, "Oh, this is just the beginning of a bad day ahead". The old voice is so faint it's barely audible. It is just there to help me appreciate how far I have come.

My negative and positive thoughts have been at war most of my life; they have constantly been in competition for my attention. After much research, I have discovered that my mind is doing its best to keep me safe. I have also discovered that our brain has some built-in and learnt default strategies that are not always helpful. My struggles have inspired me to take a closer look at myself and develop strategies that guide me to a more cohesive internal communication system, so I can create moments to hear myself with clarity. This process has enabled me to find healthier processes towards finding the balance between enjoying life and facing challenges.

One of the conflicts I came across on my journey were words and phrases like "I should", "Have to" and "How dare you". I remember thinking our whole language system needed an overhaul. Once I was able to pinpoint the pain beneath my unfavorable words and behaviours, I became more able to communicate on a level of compassion with others and myself.

Avoiding conflict, trying to constantly please others, and not recognising I was burnt out until it was too late, were all part of my automatic thought and behaviour patterns. I used to feel like no one quite understood me and that whatever I did was never good enough. I came to realise I have a choice: I can make my life into continuous stories of "good and bad", "victims, bullies and heroes" or I could try something new. Being more specific than looking for "right and wrong", means taking time to notice whether I feel healthy, safe and appreciated; this enables me to understand myself more clearly. Living by my values, setting the intention to communicate respectfully, and creating win-win resolutions have helped me find a peaceful base to reset myself from. Having an intention to connect rather than to be right or to please, has given my voice more authenticity.

Self-awareness is one of my daily practices that help to minimise my automatic reactive patterns. I am more often able to catch myself becoming uncomfortable and change my approach, before saying something I am going to regret. Taking time to meditate whilst on a walk, before bed or before I start the day, helps to increase my ability to understand myself. When I notice I haven't made time to meditate, I take regular moments to focus on my breath and check in. Nowadays, I feel less reliant on others to attend to my feelings and needs, and yet at the same time, I feel there is more appreciation and understanding between myself, my family, friends, colleagues and students.

Taking just a moment to listen to oneself beyond thoughts, with conscious breaths, can infuse us with compassion and harmony. When we treat ourselves with authenticity, compassion, respect and love, we will be more able to treat each other with the same harmonious qualities. Being open to each other's views, whilst respecting our values, will further support each other's wellbeing. Awareness of our inner-dialogue is vital towards creating a peaceful life.

Becoming the observers of our experiences helps us develop our ability to notice and take time to enjoy splashes of contentment. Equally we can notice negative moments, give ourselves space to guide our way through, knowing we will eventually come back to positive or neutral emotions. When we understand that all emotions and experiences are temporary, we can focus on directing our lives in light of our experiences.

Each of us can create our own unique supportive language as we continue to invite mindful moments into our lives. To achieve a more peaceful existence, each of us needs to be willing to listen with awareness, acceptance and compassion. Creating mindful moments has helped me weave peace and calmness into my thought processes. I hope I have supported you to create your own unique strategies towards increasing regular mindful moments to hear your inner wisdom, strength and peace.

Converting our internal world towards a peaceful existence

is something we can strive for.

If the outside world echoes, it will be a welcome bonus.

Acknowledgements

To Mum and Dad, I am thankful for the unconditional love, support and solid home you provided for Melissa, Aaron and myself. You have enabled us to enjoy life to the best of our ability and have supported us even after we left the nest, returned to the nest, and left again. We all have our own families now and I am grateful for your ongoing love, compassion and strength.

To my husband, thank you for supporting all that I do. Your love is gold and I appreciate you. Eden, in your short time on earth, you helped me discover that love knows no boundaries. Eloise, thank you for filling our days with endless fun, love and wonder.

To my husband's parents and all our extended family, your warmhearted nature and calm wisdom are a bonus to our family. Thank you for always being there for us. You enrich our hearts and our every day lives.

My dearest friend Britta, I am incredibly grateful for your strength, compassion, meticulousness, fun-loving and talented nature. You always encourage me to do my best and have faithfully supported my determination in sharing my journey into mindfulness. As we face life's highs and lows, it's great to know we can share our experiences and support each other in transforming suffering into strengths. I deeply appreciate your wisdom and friendship.

Karyn, your profound love for Whinnie and Hayden gave me the wings to have Eloise. Aaron's ability to support your wishes is equally beyond measure. I feel that Whinnie and Eden's short lives have been filled with love beyond anything we could have imagined. There are no words to capture how grateful we are for sharing your love for your family with us. With all our hearts, we are eternally grateful.

Lynne, thank you so much for being willing to assist in reading and editing this book. I deeply appreciate your willingness to trial the strategies and support me in ensuring they were effective enough to share with others. I treasure your honest, wise and insightful feedback. Thank you.

Thank you to all the staff, students, parents and community of St Christopher's Primary School for being such an inspiration from when I started in 2005. And a special thanks to Adrian for giving me the opportunity to create and share mindful experiences with students and colleagues as we all journey together in finding our inner calm, wisdom and strength.

Elizabeth, my beautiful friend, there are no words to describe your endless compassion, talent, love and strength. The song you wrote for Eden is just one of the many thoughtful gifts you gave my family. You, Matt, Lucas and Charlie have given our family so much strength and confidence to help us achieve having a family. Elizabeth, you have always believed in me, and my appreciation exceeds what I can pay forward in one lifetime. Thank you.

Genevieve, your talent, kindhearted and lovable nature are just some of the things I treasure about you. Thank you so much for being willing to paint me an artistic picture of the brain so that I could share it through this book. Really appreciate all the giggles, tears and support we are able to give each other; love our friendship.

Acknowledgements

Thank you Luke Purchase and Irene Cornerstone for allowing me to share your amazing photos from your blog *12 Moons Today*. And to Jane Power, thank you for the photos you took, you are so talented. I really appreciate your work and your friendship.

Thank you to Busybird Publishing for your amazing support and expertise. Especially Lauren for your outstanding editing skills, and to Blaise, Les and Kevin for your patience and assistance in helping me share my book. I highly recommend your team to anyone who is thinking of publishing a book.

An extended thank you to:

> Mercy Hospital for Woman, Heidelberg; The Perinatal, Consumer Advisory Committee and Pastoral Care department,
>
> IVF Melbourne Clinic, Dr Manuela Toledo and the team,
>
> Bridget Curran, D & B Health Psychologist,
>
> Christine Ellingworth, Counselling Psychologist,
>
> VARTA, Kate Bourne and the team.

About the Author

Sandra Harwood has a Bachelor in Education, Diploma in Early Childhood, and is a qualified Personal Trainer and Life Coach. Sandra currently runs a Mindfulness program for children and staff at St Christopher's Primary School. In her 27 years of teaching, Sandra has taught in all areas of the curriculum from foundation to grade six, including being an Art Specialist and Reading Recovery Specialist.

Sandra has facilitated Mindfulness and Well-Being Workshops for principals, leaders, staff and parents. She is on the Mercy Hospital for Women's Advisory Committee and has assisted in facilitating family workshops for VARTA (Victorian, Assisted Reproductive Treatment Authority). Her passion for mindfulness comes from having faced and overcome adversities and a desire to enhance our perceptions and abilities towards enjoying all life has to offer.

Recommended Resources

Books

Brené Brown, *Daring Greatly*, Penguin Putnam Inc Publishing.

Brené Brown, *The Gifts of Imperfection: Let Go of Who You Think You're Supposed to Be and Embrace Who You Are*, Hazelden Publishing.

Russ Harris, *The Happiness Trap*, Trumpeter Publishing.

Andrew Newberg M.D. and Mark Robert Waldman, *Words Can Change Your Brain*, Penguin Group Publishing.

Marshall Rosenberg PhD, *Non Violent Communication: A Language of Life*, Puddle Dancer Press.

Shauna L Shapiro, *Mindful Discipline: A Loving Approach to Setting Limits and Raising an Emotionally Intelligent Child*, New Harbinger Publications.

Daniel J Siegel, *The Whole-Brain Child*, Random House Inc. Publishing.

Eckhart Tolle, *The Power of Now*, Namaste Publishing.

Eckhart Tolle, *A New Earth*, Penguin Publishing.

Thich Nhat Hanh, *No Mud, No Lotus*, Parallax Press Publishing division of Unified Buddhist Church.

Mark Williams and Danny Penman, *Mindfulness: A Practical Guide to Finding Peace in a Frantic World*, Little, Brown Book Group Publishing.

Audio book

Dr. Rick Hanson Ph. D, *Hardwiring Happiness*, Bolinda Publishing Pty Ltd.

Websites

About Meditation, *John Kabat-Zinn on Benefits of Meditation*, Online guide for the modern meditator.

<http://aboutmeditation.com/jon-kabatzinn-on-benefits-of-meditation/>

Dr. Rick Hanson, *Taking in the Good*.

<http://www.rickhanson.net/take-in-the-good/>

Tamara Levitt, *How to Find the Calm Within the Chaos*, Begin Within.

<http://www.beginwithin.ca/bio>

Vicky Carrel & Company, *Building Confidence, Feel Capable, Achieve Success*.

<http://vikkicarrel.com>

Lecture

L Nadel, Building Brains, Creating Minds, 23 February 2010, Psychology, University of Arizona Regents.

<https://www.youtube.com/watch?v=XCrYwtnzCQA>

Videos

TED Talks, Brené Brown on Vulnerability.

<https://www.ted.com/talks/brene_brown_on_vulnerability/up-next>

TED Talks, Jill Bolte Taylor's *My Stroke of Insight*.

<https://www.ted.com/talks/jill_bolte_taylor_s_powerful_stroke_of_insight/up-next≥>

Dr. Stephen R Covey, keynote speaker and author of *The 7 Habits of Highly Effective People*.

<https://www.youtube.com/watch?v=jcTxpbRVIno>

<https://www.youtube.com/watch?v=SiNEIKx64f0>

App

Calm: Meditation to Relax, Focus & Sleep Better. *Available on the App Store, and Google Play. Compatible with Android and OS devices.*

www.ingramcontent.com/pod-product-compliance
Lightning Source LLC
Chambersburg PA
CBHW021115080526
44587CB00010B/522